Dear

Through more than fifty years of walking with God, I have often found the encouragement I needed and a fresh supply of grace in the promises of God.

His promises are as real and powerful today as they were when they were first made thousands of years ago. This booklet contains fifty promises that have been particularly meaningful in my spiritual journey. These are some of the promises that I have returned to over and over again.

In them, I have found stability in times of stress, comfort in times of loss, peace in times of doubt, and so much more. These promises have been a constant reminder of the heart and ways of the ultimate Promise Keeper.

I would encourage you to read and savor each of these promises—not just once, but repeatedly, as you need to be reminded of His covenant-keeping love and His eternal, unfailing plan and purposes.

Meditate on these promises; memorize them; make them part of your life. Use the space provided to record additional Scripture promises that God uses to strengthen your own heart. Most of all, believe His promises, for "he who promised is faithful." (Heb. 10:23).

Trusting Him,

Nancy

Nancy DeMoss Wolgemuth

God will always be our safe refuge

"The eternal God is your dwelling place, and underneath are the everlasting arms."

— DEUTERONOMY 33:27

God is our refuge and strength, a very present help in trouble. . . . The LORD of hosts is with us; the God of Jacob is our fortress.

— PSALM 46:1, 7

The LORD is your keeper. . . . The LORD will keep you from all evil; he will keep your life. The LORD will keep your going out and your coming in from this time forth and forevermore.

— PSALM 121:5, 7–8

He who dwells in the shelter of the Most High will abide in the shadow of the Almighty.

I will say to the LORD, "My refuge and my fortress, my God, in whom I trust."

He will cover you with his pinions, and under his wings you will find refuge; his faithfulness is a shield and buckler.

A thousand may fall at your side, ten thousand at your right hand, but it will not come near you.

— PSALM 91:1–2, 4, 7

The name of the LORD is a strong tower; the righteous man runs into it and is safe.

— PROVERBS 18:10

The name of the LORD is a strong tower; the righteous man runs into it and is safe.

PROVERBS 18:10

God will save us from evil and our enemies

Though I walk in the midst of trouble, you preserve my life; you stretch out your hand against the wrath of my enemies, and your right hand delivers me.

— **PSALM 138:7**

O Lord, my LORD, the strength of my salvation, you have covered my head in the day of battle.

— **PSALM 140:7**

The God of peace will soon crush Satan under your feet.

— **ROMANS 16:20**

I cry out to God Most High, to God who fulfills his purpose for me.

He will send from heaven and save me; he will put to shame him who tramples on me. Selah. God will send out his steadfast love and his faithfulness!

— **PSALM 57:2–3**

Mightier than the thunders of many waters, mightier than the waves of the sea, the LORD on high is mighty!

— **PSALM 93:4**

God will strengthen and encourage us

Fear not, for I am with you; be not dismayed, for I am your God; I will strengthen you, I will help you, I will uphold you with my righteous right hand.

— **ISAIAH 41:10**

God will strengthen and encourage us

(Continued)

"Have I not commanded you? Be strong and courageous. Do not be frightened, and do not be dismayed, for the LORD your God is with you wherever you go."

— JOSHUA 1:9

"You keep him in perfect peace whose mind is stayed on you, because he trusts in you. Trust in the LORD forever, for the LORD God is an everlasting rock."

— ISAIAH 26:3–4

They who wait for the LORD shall renew their strength; they shall mount up with wings like eagles; they shall run and not be weary; they shall walk and not faint.

— ISAIAH 40:31

"Even to your old age I am he, and to gray hairs I will carry you. I have made, and I will bear; I will carry and will save."

— ISAIAH 46:4

Wait for the LORD; be strong, and let your heart take courage; wait for the LORD!

— PSALM 27:14

God will sanctify us through and through

May the God of peace himself sanctify you completely, and may your whole spirit and soul and body be kept blameless at the coming of our LORD Jesus Christ.

He who began a good work in you will bring it to completion at the day of Jesus Christ.

— PHILIPPIANS 1:6

He who calls you is faithful; he will surely do it.

— 1 THESSALONIANS 5:23–24

Fear not, for I am with you; be not dismayed, for I am your God; I will strengthen you, I will help you, I will uphold you with my righteous right hand.

ISAIAH 41:10

God will hear and answer our humble cries

The LORD is near to all who call on him, to all who call on him in truth. He fulfills the desire of those who fear him; he also hears their cry and saves them.

— PSALM 145:18–19

The eyes of the LORD are toward the righteous and his ears toward their cry.

When the righteous cry for help, the LORD hears and delivers them out of all their troubles.

The LORD is near to the brokenhearted and saves the crushed in spirit.

Many are the afflictions of the righteous, but the LORD delivers him out of them all.

— PSALM 34:15, 17–19

"I, I am he who blots out your transgressions for my own sake, and I will not remember your sins."

ISAIAH 43:25

God will grant us mercy and forgiveness

"The mountains may depart and the hills be removed, but my steadfast love shall not depart from you, and my covenant of peace shall not be removed," says the LORD, who has compassion on you.

— **ISAIAH 54:10**

"I, I am he who blots out your transgressions for my own sake, and I will not remember your sins."

— **ISAIAH 43:25**

The LORD is merciful and gracious, slow to anger and abounding in steadfast love.

He does not deal with us according to our sins, nor repay us according to our iniquities.

For as high as the heavens are above the earth, so great is his steadfast love toward those who fear him;

As far as the east is from the west, so far does he remove our transgressions from us.

— **PSALM 103:8, 10–12**

God will give us His peace

The effect of righteousness will be peace, and the result of righteousness, quietness and trust forever.

— **ISAIAH 32:17**

Do not be anxious about anything, but in everything by prayer and supplication with thanksgiving let your requests be made known to God.

And the peace of God, which surpasses all understanding, will guard your hearts and your minds in Christ Jesus.

— **PHILIPPIANS 4:6–7**

God will bless us and make us a blessing

The righteous flourish like the palm tree and grow like a cedar in Lebanon. They are planted in the house of the LORD; they flourish in the courts of our God. They still bear fruit in old age; they are ever full of sap and green, to declare that the Lord is upright; he is my rock, and there is no unrighteousness in him.

— PSALM 92:12–15

The LORD will guide you continually and satisfy your desire in scorched places and make your bones strong; and you shall be like a watered garden, like a spring of water, whose waters do not fail.

— ISAIAH 58:11

The path of the righteous is like the light of dawn, which shines brighter and brighter until full day.

— PROVERBS 4:18

Commit your way to the LORD; trust in him, and he will act.

He will bring forth your righteousness as the light, and your justice as the noonday.

— PSALM 37:5–6

The Lord God is a sun and shield; the Lord bestows favor and honor. No good thing does he withhold from those who walk uprightly.

— PSALM 84:11

Blessed are those who dwell in your house, ever singing your praise! Selah.

Blessed are those whose strength is in you, in whose heart are the highways to Zion.

As they go through the Valley of Baca they make it a place of springs. . . .

They go from strength to strength; each one appears before God in Zion.

— PSALM 84:4–7

The path of the righteous is like the light of dawn, which shines brighter and brighter until full day.

PROVERBS 4:18

Be steadfast, immovable, always abounding in the work of the LORD, knowing that in the Lord your labor is not in vain.

1 CORINTHIANS 15:58

God will give us His wisdom

He leads the humble in what is right, and teaches the humble his way.

— **PSALM 25:9**

It is you who light my lamp; the Lord my God lightens my darkness.

— **PSALM 18:28**

If any of you lacks wisdom, let him ask God, who gives generously to all without reproach, and it will be given him.

— **JAMES 1:5**

The LORD gives wisdom; from his mouth come knowledge and understanding.

— **PROVERBS 2:6**

God will sustain and support us forever

Cast your burden on the LORD, and he will sustain you; he will never permit the righteous to be moved.

— PSALM 55:22

The LORD will not forsake his people; he will not abandon his heritage.

— PSALM 94:14

When I thought, "My foot slips," your steadfast love, O LORD, held me up. When the cares of my heart are many, your consolations cheer my soul.

— PSALM 94:18–19

The LORD is my shepherd; I shall not want. . . . Surely goodness and mercy shall follow me all the days of my life, and I shall dwell in the house of the LORD forever.

— PSALM 23:1, 6

God will reward us and lift us up

Blessed is the man who remains steadfast under trial, for when he has stood the test he will receive the crown of life, which God has promised to those who love him.

— JAMES 1:12

Wait for the LORD and keep his way, and he will exalt you to inherit the land.

— PSALM 37:34

Be steadfast, immovable, always abounding in the work of the LORD, knowing that in the LORD your labor is not in vain.

— 1 CORINTHIANS 15:58

God will reward us and lift us up

(Continued)

Let us not grow weary of doing good, for in due season we will reap, if we do not give up.

— GALATIANS 6:9

"The one who conquers, I will grant him to sit with me on my throne, as I also conquered and sat down with my Father on his throne."

— REVELATION 3:21

"Be faithful unto death, and I will give you the crown of life."

— REVELATION 2:10

God will be glorified and reign forever

All the ends of the earth shall remember and turn to the LORD, and all the families of the nations shall worship before you.

For kingship belongs to the LORD, and he rules over the nations.

— PSALM 22:27–28

All the nations you have made shall come and worship before you, O LORD, and shall glorify your name.

— PSALM 86:9

His kingdom is an everlasting kingdom, and his dominion endures from generation to generation.

— DANIEL 4:3

"The earth will be filled with the knowledge of the glory of the Lord as the waters cover the sea."

— HABAKKUK 2:14

Let us not grow weary of doing good, for in due season we will reap, if we do not give up.

GALATIANS 6:9

The promise of His coming

He who testifies to these things says, "Surely I am coming soon." . . .

The grace of the LORD Jesus be with all. Amen.

— **REVELATION 22:20–21**

Personal Promises

> God has given no pledge which He will not redeem, and encouraged no hope which He will not fulfill.
>
> My brethren, God is good. He will not forsake you: He will bear you through. There is a promise prepared for your present emergencies; and if you will believe and plead it at the mercy-seat through Jesus Christ, you shall see the hand of the Lord stretched out to help you.
>
> Everything else will fail, but His Word never will. He has been to me so faithful in countless instances that I must encourage you to trust Him. I should be ungrateful to God and unkind to you if I did not do so.
>
> _____
>
> C.H. Spurgeon
> From: Cheque Book of the Bank of Faith

Personal Promises

_____

_____

_____

_____

_____

_____

_____

_____

_____

_____

_____

_____

_____

_____

_____

_____

_____

_____

For additional copies of this booklet, visit ReviveOurHearts.com
or call 866–842–8381.